Columbus and the
New World

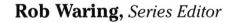

Rob Waring, *Series Editor*

HEINLE
CENGAGE Learning

Australia • Brazil • Japan • Korea • Mexico • Singapore • Spain • United Kingdom • United States

Words to Know

This story happens long ago. It starts in Europe, in the countries of Spain and Italy. It then goes across the Atlantic Ocean to a "new world."

A **The Life of Columbus.** Read the paragraph. Then match each word with the correct definition.

Christopher Columbus was a great sailor. He wanted to find a new route between Europe and Asia. At the time, some people knew that the earth was round. Columbus wanted to sail from Europe to Asia. So, he made a long voyage across the Atlantic Ocean. When he landed on a small island, Columbus thought he was in Asia. However, he was actually near a completely different continent. He was near North America. Some Europeans called this continent the 'new world' as compared to the 'old world' of Europe.

1. the earth _____

2. sail _____

3. continent _____

4. route _____

5. sailor _____

6. voyage _____

7. island _____

a. a person who sails ships as their job

b. an area of land that has water around it

c. one of the main areas of land in the world

d. the world on which we live

e. a long trip at sea

f. travel using cloth and the wind

g. the way that a person goes from one place to another

Christopher Columbus 1451–1506

B Old World Meets New World. Label the map with the correct countries.

the Bahamas	East Indies	Italy
China	India	Spain

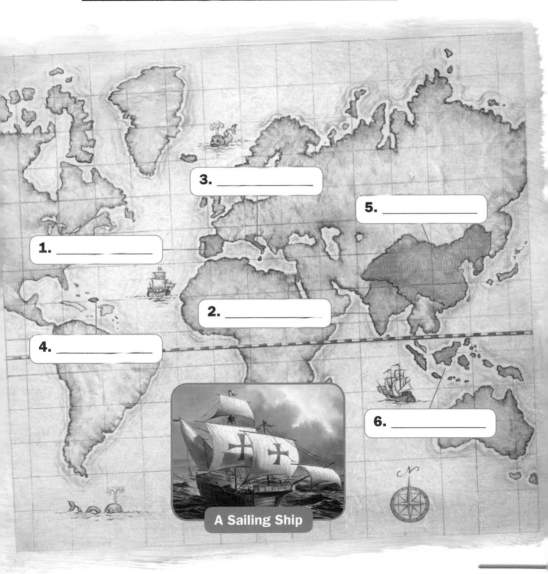

3. _____

5. _____

1. _____

2. _____

4. _____

6. _____

A Sailing Ship

Christopher Columbus was born in Italy, in 1451. The 1400s were a time of change in Europe. At that time, a lot of people in the world thought that the earth was flat. However, many educated Europeans realized that the earth was indeed round.

This possibility of a round earth changed the way that people thought. It was also of great interest to a young Columbus. When he was a young man, he decided to study **geography**.[1] He also decided to go to sea. Columbus wanted to find the answer to a major geographical problem.

------

[1]**geography:** the study of the countries of the world and the parts of the earth.

🎧 CD 2, Track 03

At the time, Europeans wanted **spices**[2] from India and China. However, it cost too much money to carry these products from the East using the traditional land and sea routes.

Columbus decided that he wanted to find a new sea route from Europe to Asia. He knew that the earth was round. Because of this, Columbus thought he could reach the East by sailing west. However, he also knew that sailing around the world would be costly. Therefore, he needed a lot of money to find out if he was right.

---

[2]**spice:** a material used to make food taste good

In 1492, Columbus **persuaded**[3] King Ferdinand and Queen Isabella of Spain to give him the money for the voyage. He received enough money for three small ships: the Nina, the Pinta, and the Santa Maria.

Columbus finally had his ships. He also had big hopes for his new sea route from Europe to Asia. Columbus and his group sailed west, but they didn't know what was waiting for them.

---

[3]**persuade:** make someone agree to do something by talking to them a lot about it

Sequence the Events

What is the correct order of the events? Number 1 to 4.

_____ Columbus received money from the King and Queen of Spain for his voyage.

_____ Columbus studied geography.

_____ Columbus sailed west.

_____ Columbus decided to find a new sea route between Europe and Asia.

The voyage was very long. On October 9, after a month at sea, the sailors were very **tired of**[4] looking for land. They wanted to go back to Europe. Finally, Columbus agreed. He said that they would look for land for three more days. If there was still no land, they would go back to Europe.

Then, just three days later, on October 12, 1492, a sailor on the Pinta **cried out**.[5] He could see land!

---

[4]**tired of:** tired and wanting to stop something
[5]**cry out:** say something loudly

At the time, Columbus didn't know what land they were seeing. People now think the land was actually a small island in the Bahamas. It was probably the one that is now known as San Salvador.

Columbus and his sailors got into a small **boot**[6] and went to the island. There, after months at sea, they got out of the boat and finally walked onto land. The land that would one day be called 'the Americas.'

---

[6]**boat:** a small vehicle for traveling on water

However, Columbus didn't realize that he was on a new continent. He believed that he and his sailors were near the coast of Asia. He thought they were in the islands of the East Indies. He even called the island people who came to meet him 'Indians.' Because of this, people incorrectly called **Native Americans**[7] 'Indians' for hundreds of years.

Columbus returned to Spain. He brought **gold**,[8] **parrots**,[9] and other things from the New World to show the king and queen. For him, this was the high point of his life as a sailor. As a result of his voyage, he was considered by some to be a very important man in Europe.

North America

---

[7] **Native Americans:** certain groups of people who first lived in North and South America
[8] **gold:** a valuable, shiny yellow metal
[9] **parrot:** a bird from hot countries which can sometimes talk

parrot

gold

Europe

Africa

South
America

Columbus brought parrots,
gold and other items from
the new world to the old.

After his big voyage, Columbus didn't just stay in Europe. During his life, he made three more voyages to the new world. But in the end, he didn't achieve what he really wanted to do. He never found a new route to bring spices from Asia to Europe. Columbus was a **disappointed**[10] man when he died on May 20, 1506. However, questions about what Columbus achieved didn't end with his death.

---

[10] **disappointed:** unhappy because something was not as good as hoped or expected

There are still concerns about Columbus's voyage today. For hundreds of years, people believed that Columbus was the first European to reach the Americas. However, people now know that the **Vikings**[11] reached North America five hundred years earlier than Columbus did. It is true that Columbus found a new world for Europeans to **explore**.[12] However, in the end, this exploration caused a number of problems for Native Americans.

Columbus made 1492 one of the most important years in world history. However, this importance was for both good and bad reasons. One thing is certain however: on October 12, 1492, the new world—and the old—changed for all time.

_____

[11] **Vikings:** groups of people from Northern Europe who traveled by sea between the 700s and 1000s
[12] **explore:** look for and find

Scan for Information

Scan page 18 to find the information.

1. Who reached North America first?

2. What was one good effect of Columbus's voyage?

3. What was one bad effect of Columbus's voyage?

After You Read

1. In paragraph 1 on page 4, 'educated' means:
   A. rich
   B. informed
   C. mistaken
   D. young

2. In paragraph 1 on page 7, the phrase 'these products' refers to:
   A. most people
   B. sea routes
   C. spices
   D. India and China

3. Why did Columbus want to sail west?
   A. to bring spices to Europe
   B. to answer a problem
   C. to get to the East
   D. all of the above

4. In paragraph 1 on page 11, the expression 'at sea' means:
   A. searching
   B. waiting
   C. sailing
   D. looking

5. Which is NOT a good heading for page 11?
   A. Columbus Returns to Europe
   B. Pinta Sailor Sees Land
   C. Sailors Getting Bored at Sea
   D. After Three More Days

6. Columbus sailed a small boat _____ the island.
   A. under
   B. in
   C. on
   D. to

7. Why did Columbus call the Native American people 'Indians'?
   A. They were from the East Indies.
   B. He misunderstood his location.
   C. He thought he was in India.
   D. He named them after the queen.

8. According to page 17, how many times did Columbus go to the new world in all?
   A. 4
   B. 3
   C. 2
   D. 1

9. According to page 18, how long before Columbus did the Vikings reach the new world?
   A. 1442 years
   B. 992 years
   C. 500 years
   D. 100 years

10. In paragraph 1 on page 18, the phrase 'a number of problems' can be replaced by:
    A. a lot of problems
    B. 1 or 2 problems
    C. a few problems
    D. much problems

11. What does the writer think about Columbus?
    A. He was a happy man.
    B. He did a bad thing.
    C. He did a good thing.
    D. He changed the world.

Class: Geography

Teacher: Ms. Lopez

Assignment: Write about a well-known ocean voyage. Describe the person who planned it and explain the purpose of it.

The Kon-Tiki
by Elliot Park

When Thor Heyerdahl was a little boy, he hoped to see the world. He wanted to learn about, and visit, unusual places all over Earth. At the age of 24, he and his wife went to live on a Polynesian island in the Pacific Ocean. He became very interested in the people who lived there. He was also interested in how these people had arrived there. Most scientists believed that these people originally came from the Asian continent. However, Heyerdahl began to think that they might have come from South America. He wanted to persuade others that his idea was right. In order to do this, he decided to sail from South America to the Polynesian Islands to prove it was possible.

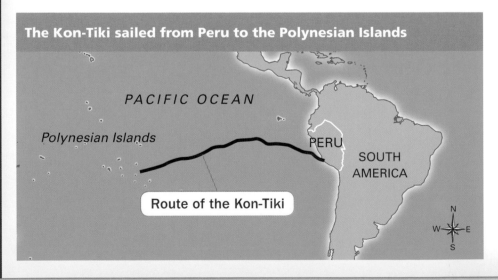

The Kon-Tiki sailed from Peru to the Polynesian Islands

PACIFIC OCEAN

Polynesian Islands

PERU

SOUTH AMERICA

Route of the Kon-Tiki

The Kon-Tiki was a large raft

Heyerdahl built a special type of boat called a 'raft.' He named it the 'Kon-Tiki.' It was the type of boat that people used to sail across the ocean centuries ago. It did not have an engine. It was made of wood and had several sails. Heyerdahl and five other men left Peru on April 28, 1947. They sailed west across the Pacific Ocean. Their voyage lasted for one hundred and one days and their route was very long. They finally arrived at the Polynesian Islands on August 7, 1947.

The voyage proved that people could sail from South America to the Polynesian Islands. However, most scientists still don't agree with Heyerdahl's idea. They don't believe that the people of Polynesia are from South America. According to them, most scientific research says differently. They argue that people from the Polynesian Islands do not have a lot in common with people from South America. They think they have more in common with people from Asia.

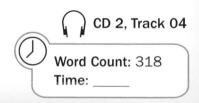

CD 2, Track 04

Word Count: 318
Time: _____

Vocabulary List

boat (12)
continent (2, 14)
cry out (11)
disappointed (17)
earth (2, 4, 7)
explore (18)
geography (4, 9)
gold (14)
island (2, 12, 14)
parrot (14)
persuade (8)
route (2, 7, 8, 9, 17)
sail (2, 7, 8, 9)
sailor (2, 11, 12, 14)
spice (7, 17)
tired of (11)
voyage (2, 8, 9, 11, 14, 17)